*gli *speciali*]

i *libri* di **artedossier**

Editorial manager
Claudio Pescio

Editing
Francesca Barberotti
Dario Dondi

Translations
Catherine Frost

Design and Layout
Lorenzo Pacini

Image Supervisor
Nicola Dini

Texts are taken from: G. Fossi, *Uffizi Gallery. Art, History, Collections*, Giunti, Firenze 2001; G. Fossi, *The Uffizi. The Official Guide*, Giunti, Firenze 1998.

© 2011 Ministero per i Beni e le Attività Culturali - Soprintendenza Speciale per il Patrimonio Storico, Artistico ed Etnoantropologico e per il Polo Museale della città di Firenze

© 2011 Giunti Editore S.p.A.
via Bolognese 165 - 50139 Florence, Italy
via Borgogna 5 - 20122 Milan, Italy

First edition: October 2011

www.giunti.it

"FIRENZE MUSEI"
is a registered trademark created by Sergio Bianco

No part of this pubblication may be reproduced in any form.

Reprint	Years
6 5 4 3 2 1	2015 2014 2013 2012

Printed by Giunti Industrie Grafiche S.p.A. – Prato (Italy), with certification FSC®

Gloria Fossi

Uffizi Gallery
The Masterpieces

GIUNTI FIRENZE MVSEI artedossier

Caravaggio, *Medusa*, oil on canvas on wooden shield poplar, diam. 55 cm, c. 1597.
[CARAVAGGIO'S ROOM]

Contents

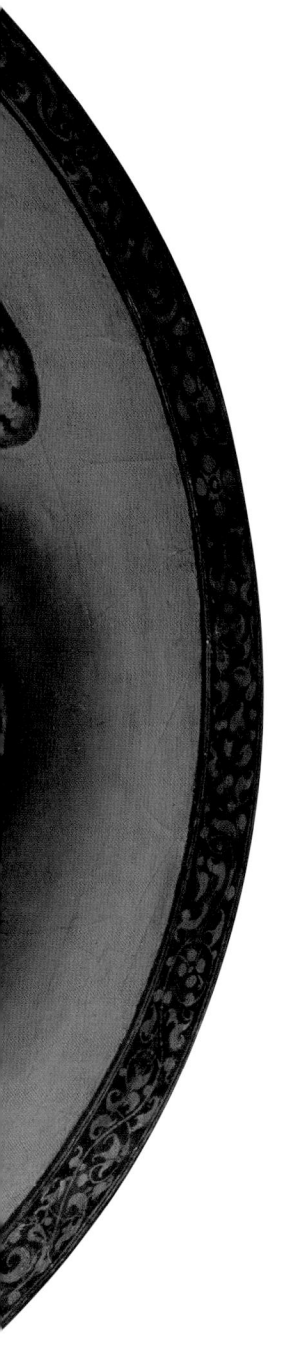

«Pictures, statues and other precious things» 6

First Corridor 10

Second and Third corridors 11

Giotto and the XIII Century 12

The XIV Century 14

The XV Century 16

The Renaissance in Northern Europe 32

The XVI Century 38

The XVII and the XVIII Centuries 50

"Pictures, statues and other precious things"

One of the world's most important museums, the Uffizi Gallery was one of the first in Europe to emerge in accordance with the modern idea of a museum, that is to say as a systematically organised exhibition space designed for public viewing.

The origins of the oldest museum in Modern Europe date back to 1581. In that year Francesco I de' Medici set up a Gallery "with pictures, statues and other precious things" on the last floor of the East Wing of the Uffizi. Nearby was the Tribuna, completed in 1584 for Francesco I by Bernardo Buontalenti. The strikingly unusual octagonal room was the heart of the original museum and displayed the most amazing objects in the fabulous Medicean collections. The imposing building complex of the Uffizi had not, on the other hand, been created as a museum. The building ordered by Cosimo I in 1560 was designed to house the Magistrature, or administrative and judiciary offices, the *uffizi* (the derivation of the name Uffizi). To design and supervise this great project Cosimo had called upon the artist and architect Giorgio Vasari from Arezzo. Vasari died in 1574, and the Uffizi was finished by Bernardo Buontalenti.

The Uffizi has a U-shaped layout consisting of two long wings, to the east and the west, joined on the southern side by a body facing the river with an airy loggia on the first floor and a portico on the ground floor opening onto the square. The East Wing is linked by an overhead passageway to Palazzo Vecchio. The West Wing is connected to the Loggia dei Lanzi by a bridge suspended over Via Lambertesca. A grandiose, imposing edifice, built to a serial design for the different Magistratures, the Uffizi was constructed of the typical Florentine material, pietra serena, which stands out against the light-toned plaster.

From March to September 1565, Vasari built, for the wedding of Francesco I and Joan of Austria, the spectacular hall known today as the Vasari Corridor, which joins the Uffizi to Palazzo Pitti. An urban project of highest symbolic significance in the city of the Grand Duke, the Corridor, almost a kilometer long, was reserved exclusively to the Medici family and high dignitaries of their court.

First Corridor

The East Corridor reflects substantially its late 16th century appearance, conceived by Francesco I, founder of the Gallery. The restoration of the corridor and its display of statues and paintings (1996) is based amongst other things upon the drawings of the Gallery carried out by Fra Benedetto de Greyss between 1748 and 1765. Following the categories defined in 1597 by the erudite Filippo Pigafetta, the older portraits from the so-called Giovio Series, partly restored, have been placed under the ceiling, which is decorated with grotesque motifs. The series depicts famous men from every age and country, and was begun for Cosimo I by Cristofano dell'Altissimo (doc. 1552-c. 1605), who in Como copied the renowned collection by Paolo Giovio. They then passed from the Pitti Palace to the Uffizi in 1587. After more than two centuries, the large three-quarter-length portraits of the Aulic series are now set back in regular spaces beneath the Giovio Series. Francesco I and his successors commissioned these to extol their family, beginning with the founder, Giovanni di Bicci. They were inspired by older prototypes. Ancient busts and sculptures from the Medici collection alternate along the walls. The ceilings with grotesque decoration were executed by a group of painters led by Alessandro Allori (Antonio Tempesta, Ludovico Buti, Giovan Maria Butteri and Ludovico Cigoli, some of whom were already active in the Studiolo of Palazzo Vecchio). The pavement in large white and grey marble squares dates back to the Lorraine period (18th century).

Second and Third Corridors

The rearrangement of the Second and Third Corridors was carried out at the same time as the restoration of the First Corridor in 1996. With its large glass windows facing the Uffizi Square and the Arno River, the South Corridor is famous for its views. Among the sculptures exhibited are the head of the so-called *Dying Alexander* from the Hellenistic period and the Roman copy of *Cupid and Psyche*. At the intersection with the East Corridor, the ceilings are painted with frescoes in the grotesque style, dating back to Francesco I (1581). Those facing west show the glorification of the Medici family and date back to Cosimo III (1670-1723). Above the windows facing the river are the later portraits of the Giovio Series, which continue into the Third Corridor together with canvas paintings from the 17th to the beginning of the 19th century, spaced alternately with the larger paintings from the Aulic Series. On the side of the doors of the Third Corridor hang c. 50 portraits of the late 18th century. The famous *Roman Wild Boar* has been reinstalled at the end of the corridor towards the Loggia dei Lanzi. This, along with the small replica of a *Farnese Hercules*, is placed beside the *Laocoon* by Baccio Bandinelli (1523), the first copy from the original of the Hellenistic group found in Rome in 1506.

Florentine School, *Grotesque Decoration with coats of arms of the Austrian dynasty Medici and of Bianca Cappello*, fresco with tempera retouches, c. 616 × 616 cm, c. 1581.

On the opposite page, Alessandro Allori, *Grotesque Decorations with Medicean Devices*, fresco with tempera retouches, 385 × 585 cm, 1581.

GIOTTO AND THE XIII CENTURY

The first room in the Uffizi is dominated by three great altarpieces, crucially important for the development of Italian medieval painting. They are the work of Tuscan artists who, in the late 13th century, were already famous beyond the boundaries of Florence: the Sienese Duccio di Boninsegna (c. 1260 - 1318), the Florentine Cimabue (1240 ? - documented up to 1302) and Giotto (c. 1267 - 1337), a native of Mugello, north of Florence, traditionally considered the pupil of Cimabue. The three colossal Maestà by the greatest masters of the late 13th century and, in the case of Giotto, the first decades of the 14th as well, were all painted between 1280 and 1310 for Florentine churches. They exemplify a laborious development that was to blossom into a 'new' art, as recognized already by the artists' contemporaries, capable of rivalling the highest figurative achievements of antiquity. Giotto, who like the ancients depicted reality with remarkable verisimilitude, was revolutionary also in his representation of pictorial space, clearly three-dimensional in the great Uffizi *Maestà*; his figures appear solidly volumetric for the first time. Not by chance, the two earlier altarpieces by Cimabue and Duccio hang almost as confrontation in this room. It was the work of these two artists, in fact, that provided the bases for Giotto's experimentation.

Cimabue,
Maestà
of Santa Trinita,
tempera on wood,
425 × 243 cm,
datable between 1280
and 1290.
[ROOM 2]

Duccio di Boninsegna,
Maestà (*Rucellai Madonna*),
tempera on wood,
450 × 293 cm,
c. 1285.
[ROOM 2]

Giotto,
The Ognissanti Madonna,
tempera on wood,
325 × 204 cm,
c. 1310.
[ROOM 2]

The XIV Century

Tuscan 14th-century painting is represented at the Uffizi by the great masters who, within a few decades' time, radically changed the traditional figurative modes. Their influence was not limited to Florence and Siena alone, the two cities that won cultural supremacy over Pisa and Lucca in the 14th century, but extended to Rome, Assisi, Padua, Rimini and Naples as well. Two paintings representing two different currents are shown here: on the one hand, the work of the Sienese artists Simone Martini (c. 1284 - 1344) and Lippo Memmi (documented from 1317 to 1344), more inclined than the Florentines to a rich, refined manner, abounding in minute detail; and on the other, the pictorial style of Florentines such as Giottino (att. second half of the 14th century), strongly influenced by Giotto, who had depicted personages with concrete, realistically human expressions, and an emphasis on basic forms rather than details. The famous *Annunciation* comes from the Siena Cathedral. Painted by Simone Martini in collaboration with his brother-in-law Lippo Memmi, it dates from 1333, a time prior to the artist's stay in France, at Avignon. It was the first of the medieval panel paintings to arrive at the Gallery, in 1799. Typically Sienese in its refined use of gold and the accentuated linearism of the Virgin's graceful, flowing gesture of withdrawal, the *Annunciation* displays such elegant, realistic details as the varied patterns of the marble flooring, the angel's chequered mantle, the vase of lilies and the foreshortened view of the half-open book. The angel's words of greeting to the Virgin, appearing in a kind of comic-strip balloon, are dramatically effective. Standing at the sides of the Annunciation are St. Ansanus and St. Giulitta (or Margaret). In the medallions above appear the prophets Jeremiah, Ezekiel, Isaiah and Daniel, with scrolls alluding to the Incarnation (the central roundel, now lost, above the dove of the Holy Spirit, must have portrayed God the Father).

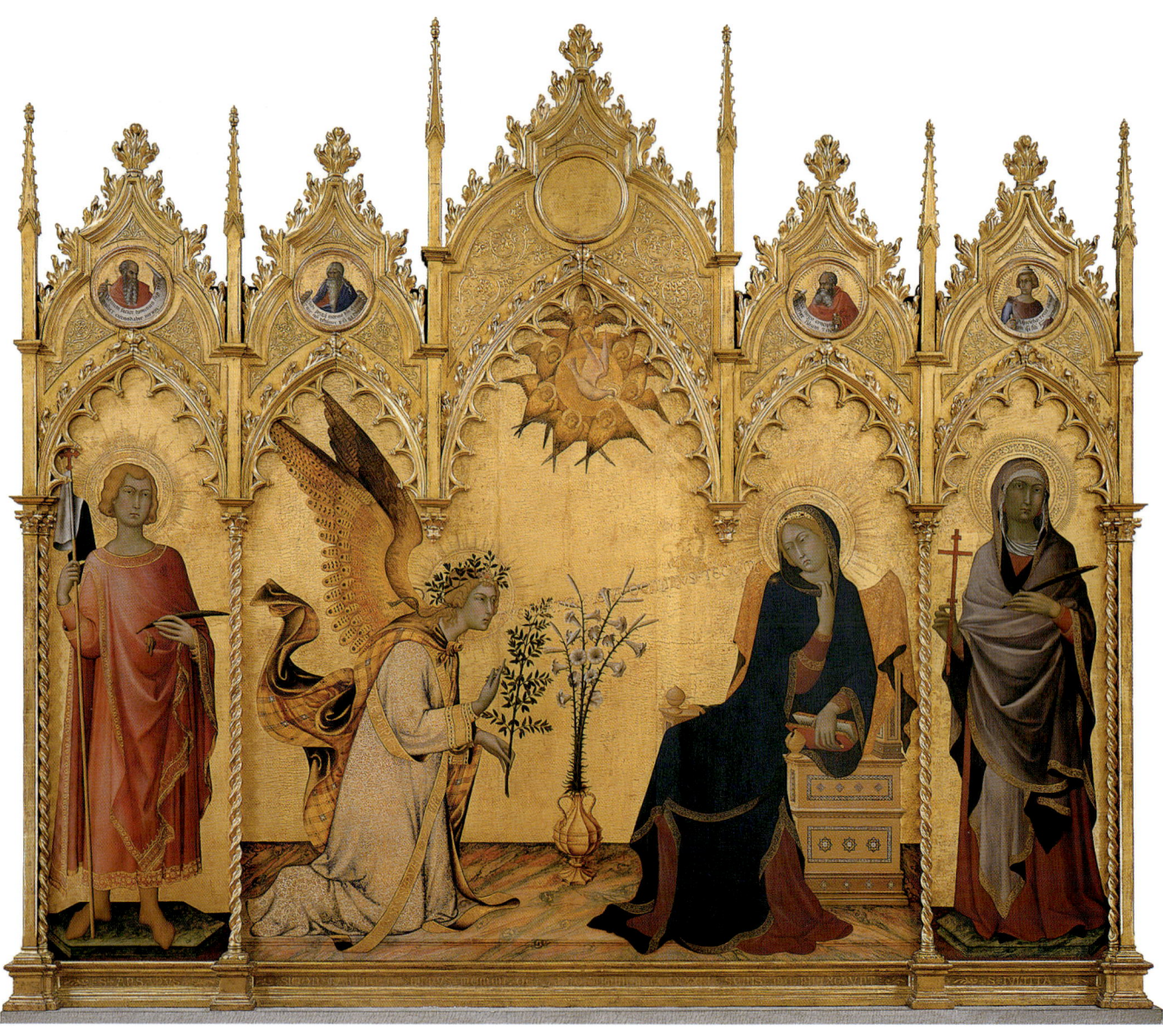

Giottino's *Pietà* is instead a masterpiece of Florentine painting from the second half of the 14th century, outstanding for the unusual psychological analysis of the faces and the luminous pictorial effect. In addition to the traditional personages of a *Lamentation for the Dead Christ*, there are two women in contemporary dress: a Benedictine nun and a sumptuously gowned young woman, kneeling to witness the sorrowful event under the protective hands of the Patron Saints, Benedict and Remigious.

Giottino,
Pietà,
tempera on wood,
195 × 134 cm,
c. 1360-1365,
whole and detail.
[ROOM 4]

On the opposite page,
Simone Martini
and Lippo Memmi,
Annunciation,
tempera on wood,
184 × 210 cm,
1333.
[ROOM 3]

The XV Century

The collection of 15th century Italian paintings, among the Uffizi's most famous, owes its prestige to the numerous works by Florentine artists, including the world's largest group of paintings by Botticelli, Filippo and Filippino Lippi. There are also many masterpieces from the schools of Northern and Central Italy, as well as dozens of paintings still in storage. The main core consists of about a hundred paintings exhibited in nine rooms in the Western wing of the building. The *Santa Lucia dei Magnoli Altarpiece* by Domenico Veneziano (c. 1410 - 1461) presents an innovative use of light makes it one of the masterpieces of its time. That Sacred Conversation takes place within a harmonious architectural structure of three arches with inlaid marble on the façade, rendered still more delicate by the pastel tones of rose and green, and enriched by a multicoloured pavement in receding squares. The morning light is emphasised by the shadow falling on the Virgin and Child. The branches of a citrus orchard stand out against an intensely realistic sky, no more golden and abstract as the paintings of the

Gothic period. In the foreground are St Francis, St John the Baptist, St Zanobius (patron of Florence, wearing a rich costume with fabric and jewels of the era) and St Lucia, to whom the church was dedicated.

Fundamental to the evolution of early Renaissance painting is *Saint Anne Metterza*. This work was the fruit of a collaboration between Masolino (1383-1440) and his younger countryman Masaccio (1401-1428 ?). St Anne and the angels are generally attributed to Masolino, except for the one on the top right of the painting, probably done by Masaccio, who was also responsible for the Virgin with Child. The symbolic meaning of this altarpiece is, despite the simplicity of its composition, quite complex. It is not known under what circumstances the work was commissioned. The three main figures, St Anne, the Virgin, and the Child, placed along the same axis, have the static quality of Byzantine Madonnas (but the plasticity of the figures is entirely 15th century, and the angel swinging the censer introduces a sense of movement).

On the opposite page, Domenico Veneziano, *Santa Lucia dei Magnoli Altarpiece* (*Madonna and Child enthroned between Saints Francis, John the Baptist, Zenobius and Lucia*), tempera on wood, 209 × 216 cm, c. 1440-1445.
[ROOM 7]

Masaccio e Masolino, *Saint Anne Metterza*, tempera on wood, 175 × 103 cm, c. 1424.
[ROOM 7]

With its rich use of gold, applied to the panel in relief at certain points, the *Adoration of the Magi* by Gentile da Fabriano (c. 1370 - 1427) has in the The Adoration at the centre of the panel the culminating moment of the fabulous procession of the Magi, which winds its way down from the top of the panel. The eye is drawn to many details: from the numerous flowers, all drawn from nature, to the small pillars, to the fabrics woven with gold, and the harnesses of the horses. This analytical intensity of detail would seem to correspond to the literary style typical of Greek humanism, the so-called *ekphrasis*, which allows the minute, elaborate description of multiple elements.

Gentile da Fabriano,
Adoration of the Magi,
tempera on wood,
halos and friezes
stamped with iron,
300 × 283 cm (total),
173 × 220 cm (panel),
c. 1423, whole and detail
on the opposite page.
[ROOM 5-6]

Paolo Uccello,
The Battle of San Romano,
tempera on wood,
181 x 323 cm, c. 1438-1440.
[ROOM 7]

The famous *Urbino Diptych*, by Piero della Francesca (c. 1412 - 1492), painted on both sides, was probably joined by a hinge to be opened like a book. The precision of the features, focusing even on less attractive details (such as Federigo's unforgettable nose, broken during a tournament), is typical of Flemish art and confirms that Piero della Francesca, active at the court of Urbino, was one of the most sensitive interpreters of Nordic art, well-known and appreciated at that time from Ferrara to Florence, from Urbino to Southern Italy. Even the crystal-clear landscape in the background, fading towards the distant hills and the horizon, possibly evoking the territory of Montefeltro, the Duke's land, is treated with an almost miniaturist technique. Without the traditional expedient of a curtain or window, the magnificent bird's-eye view unites the perspective of the two panels. Contemporary to the *Diptych* by Piero della Francesca, is the *Portrait of a Woman* variously assigned to Antonio del Pollaiolo (c. 1431 - 1498) or to his brother Piero (c. 1441 - 1496). The woman is portrayed in a half-bust profile on a rich background of blue lapis lazuli. Around her neck is a pearl necklace with a particularly beautiful pendent, which shows an angel in relief overlying a large ruby. She is wearing a head-dress typical of 15th century Florentine ladies: a veil covers her ears and the "honeycomb" plait in her golden hair is delicately highlighted by pearls.

Piero della Francesca,
Diptych of the Duke and Duchess of Urbino,
front panels with the portraits of Battista Sforza and Federigo II da Montefeltro,
tempera on wood,
47 × 33 cm each,
c. 1465-1472.
[ROOM 22]

On the opposite page,
Antonio or Piero del Pollaiolo,
Portrait of a Woman,
tempera on wood,
55 × 34 cm,
c. 1475.
[ROOM 9]

This famous altarpiece by Sandro Botticelli (1445-1510) is a public homage to Lorenzo the Magnificent and his family, with whom Botticelli was in contact. Against a backdrop of ancient ruins a favourite scene of the Medici is shown – the procession through the streets in which they took part every year with the Confraternity of Magi, dressed as oriental kings. Apart from the self-portrait of Botticelli which stares at the viewer from the right of the painting, Giuliano de' Medici stands out on the left; leaning on him is the poet Poliziano with Pico della Mirandola beside him. The Magus kneeling at the feet of Jesus is Cosimo the Elder, whilst the king with the red cloak seen from behind is Piero the Gouty, the father of Lorenzo (seen in profile on the right, with a short black garment).

Sandro Botticelli,
Adoration of the Magi,
tempera on wood,
111 × 134 cm,
c. 1475.
[ROOM 10-14]

On the opposite page,
Domenico Ghirlandaio,
*Madonna Enthroned
with Child, Angels
and Saints*,
tempera on wood,
190 × 200 cm,
c. 1484-1486.
[ROOM 10-14]

Very sensitive to Flemish art, Domenico Ghirlandaio (1449-1494), a talented portrait painter, who drew inspiration from it for landscapes and for a special attention to decorative details, created the *Madonna Enthroned with Child, Angels and Saints*. Against the background of a crystal clear sky, a balustrade covered in jewels supports the enthroned Virgin, surrounded by four garlanded angels – a composition which had become well-established in Florence by this period. The Child is blessing San Giusto, the patron saint of the church, who kneels at the front of the painting. The other figures are archangels Michael and Raphael, standing, and St Zanobius, patron saint of Florence, kneeling on the right. Standing out against the landscape are cypresses, a hibiscus and an orange tree. Vasari praised the metallic brilliance of the Archangel Michael's armour, obtained not through the application of gold, but with pure colour, an innovation first attributable to this artist.

Sandro Botticelli's *Primavera* is perhaps the most famous painting in the Uffizi. The complex allegory seems to have been inspired by the classical texts of Ovid and Lucretius and by certain verses of Agnolo Poliziano, friend of the Medici and of the artist, who in the *Stanze* written for the tournament of Giuliano de' Medici (1475) describes a garden with the Three Graces and the springtime wind Zephyrus chasing after Flora. This interpretation seems to be confirmed particularly by the winged genie on the right of the painting, considered to be Zephyrus who chased and possessed the nymph Chloris and then married her, giving her the gift of germinating flowers. Beside Chloris stands the smiling figure clothed in flowers, one of the most memorable women in the history of art, who represents, according to this explanation, the transformation of Chloris into Flora, the Latin goddess of Spring. The woman in the center is possibly Venus, and this is her garden. The three women on the left entwined in a dance, derived from ancient images of the Three Graces, may be the symbol of Liberality. Above is Cupid, the blindfolded God of love. Finally, the youth with a traveler's hat, sword and winged sandals is certainly Mercury, herald of Jove, who perhaps appears here as an emblem of knowledge. According to the most widely accepted hypotheses, the allegory of Spring, the season in which the invisible world of Form descends to mould and shape Matter, may be celebrating the marriage in 1482 of the erudite Lorenzo di Pierfrancesco de' Medici, friend of Botticelli, and Semiramide Appiani, a relative of Simonetta Vespucci, famous for her beauty and for her presumed liaison with Giuliano de' Medici. In a more recent interpretation, however, the philologist Claudia Villa (1998) has viewed the painting as a metaphorical celebration of the Liberal Arts. In any case, Botticelli's allegory remains one of the highest expressions of an ideal return to the Golden Age in the Florence of Lorenzo the Magnificent.

Sandro Botticelli is also the author of *The Birth of Venus* narrating a different episode from the legend of the goddess: her arrival at the island of Kythera or perhaps Cyprus. Against a seascape rendered with the utmost mastery, Venus stands naked on a huge shell, being pushed towards shore by the swell of the sea, helped by the breath of the winds Zephyrus and Aura who embrace softly whilst roses fall from the sky. She is welcomed by a girl wearing a silken cloak embroidered with daisies and other flowers: this is possibly the Hora of Spring or one of the Three Graces. Like the *Primavera*, this famous work is representative of the most serene and graceful phase of Botticelli's art, linked to the neo-Platonic atmosphere of Lorenzo's age.

Sandro Botticelli,
Primavera,
oil tempera on wood,
203 x 314 cm,
c. 1482, whole and detail
on the opposite page.
[ROOM 10-14]

On the following pages,
Sandro Botticelli,
The Birth of Venus,
tempera on linen canvas,
172.5 x 278.5 cm,
c. 1484.
[ROOM 10-14]

New hypotheses for the reading of the *Annunciation* by Leonardo da Vinci (1452-1519) have been stimulated by its restoration, completed in March 2000, which has revealed not only its luminosity and clarity of detail but a stronger sense of perspective in the architectural foreshortening on the right (the door, of which both doorjambs can now be seen, gives a clearer glimpse of the baldachin in the room). In some details the influence of Verrocchio, or perhaps Leonardo's homage to his master, can be recognized (especially in the base supporting the lectern, reminiscent of the Sepulcher of Giovanni and Piero de' Medici in San Lorenzo). The Virgin's arm seems disproportionately elongated, unable to reach the book on the lectern, and the angel's shadow is too dark for the light of dawn, which restoration has shown to be the hour chosen by Leonardo da Vinci as the setting, perhaps with symbolic overtones, for the Annunciation. The meadow is sprinkled with a myriad of flowers studied from life; in the beautiful landscape, typical Tuscan cypresses trail off into the distance where the minute details of a lake-side city blend into the bluish tones of the bare rocky mountains in the background.

Leonardo da Vinci, *Annunciation*, oil tempera on wood, 98 x 217 cm, c. 1475-1480.
[ROOM 15]

The Renaissance in Northern Europe

Among the important group of Flemish, Dutch and German paintings from the 15th and 16th centuries, many of them documented in Florence very early, the oldest is Rogier van der Weyden's splendid *Deposition in the Sepulcher*. The veduta in the background is typically Nordic in its minute detail, showing how the Flemish, now well-acquainted with Italian style, were able to adopt it to express emotions, but without abandoning their own perception of the world, viewed as a sort of microcosm. Such suggestions did not flow in one direction only. The Italians too, fascinated by the minutely realistic, almost sensual, interpretation of nature offered by the Nordic masters – the first to confer incomparable brilliancy and transparency on their works through the oil technique – drew inspiration from them, while retaining a style imbued with the ideals of harmony and formal perfection deriving from the study of antiquity and linear perspective. The fertile exchange between the two main figurative currents of the early 15th century, continuing throughout the century and beyond, was also favored by a fortunate set of circumstances. Living in Bruges at the time was a substantial community of merchants and bankers, many of them from Florence and Lucca. In the flourishing center that was the residence of the Dukes of Burgundy, Jan van Eyck, founder of the Flemish school, had worked up to 1441, and later Hans Memling and his followers, among them the excellent Gérard David. Near the end of the century German artists too began to approach Italian art, inspired by it and influencing it in turn, through the growing popularity of engravings. First among them was the great Dürer, who studied the works of Mantegna, Giovanni Bellini and Leonardo in Venice. Some masterpieces from his youth and his maturity are displayed at the Uffizi, as well as two heads of Apostles from 1516, donated in 1620 by the Emperor Ferdinando II to Cosimo II de' Medici.

Rogier van der Weyden, *Deposition in the Sepulcher*, oil on oak wood, 111 x 95 cm, c. 1460-1463, whole and detail on the opposite page.
[ROOM 10-14]

The grandiose *Portinari Triptych* by Hugo Van der Goes (c. 1440 - 1482), is of crucial importance for the appreciation of Flemish art in Florence in the late 15th century. In this triptych the backs of the side panels too are painted with an *Annunciation in grisaille*, as was traditional with the great Flemish altarpieces composed of several closable leafs; on the front the panels were decorated with monochrome images resembling living statues. In the central panel the *Adoration of the Shepherds*, rich in symbolical allusions, shines as if by moonlight amid the scenario of the ruined temple of David, whose lyre appears in the lunette on the portal. On the side panels are the patrons: at left Tommaso Portinari and his two eldest sons, Antonio (born in 1472) and Pigello (born in 1474). Behind them are their guardian saints Anthony Abbot and Thomas. To the right, deep in prayer, protected by the saint for whom she is named, is Tommaso's wife Maria Maddalena Baroncelli, married in 1470 when she was sixteen, by whom he had ten children. Beside her is her daughter Maria (born around 1471), by some thought to be Margherita, the name of the guardian saint crushing the dragon behind her.

Hugo van der Goes,
The Portinari Triptych
(*Adoration of the
Shepherds with
the Patrons and
Guardian Saints*),
oil on wood,
253 x 304 cm (central panel),
253 x 141 cm (side panels),
c. 1477-1478.
[ROOM 10-14]

On the opposite page,
Hugo van der Goes,
Portinari Triptych
(*Adoration of the
Shepherds with
the Patrons and
Guardian Saints*),
oil on wood,
c. 1477-1478,
detail of the right
side panel.
[ROOM 10-14]

The *Adoration of the Magi* painted by Albrecht Dürer, which may have been accompanied by side panels, was finished slightly before Dürer's departure for his second voyage to Italy. In its intense colors and its perspective the work reflects the Venetian painting studied by Dürer on his first trip in 1494, especially that of Mantegna and Giovanni Bellini, by whom Dürer was warmly welcomed to Venice in 1506. The ancient ruins inspired by Italian art are combined here with a landscape and distant figures of Nordic taste. Careful analysis of plants and animals, rich in symbolic meaning, documents the practice of studying from life distinctive of many of the German master's works.

Albrecht Dürer,
Adoration of the Magi,
oil on wood,
99 x 113.5 cm,
1504.
[ROOM 20]

The XVI Century

The 16th century is by definition the "Golden Age" of Italian painting, and not in Florence alone. Over the years Florence had been slowly losing the cultural supremacy it had enjoyed since the days of the Republic, guided by the Gonfaloniere Pier Soderini. At that time Florence saw such masters as Leonardo, Michelangelo (1475-1564) and the young Raphael (1483-1520) at work on great projects. In this period painters traveled often to Rome, frequently staying for years. In the city of the Popes the most complex and ambitious artistic experimentation was being carried out in the early decades of the 16th century. Love of antiquity was still intense, and the sensational findings then being unearthed – like the disinterment of the Hellenistic group called the *Laocoon* in January of 1506 – exerted an irresistible appeal. Before the dramatic events of the Sack (1527), the Urbe lived one of its finest cultural seasons. While the pope's court welcomed and honored painters from all over Italy, an important role was also played by patrons of art such as the "magnificent" Agostino Chigi (1465-1520). In addition to Michelangelo and Raphael, who had left Florence for some time now – where art was not still in decline due to the presence of masters such as Pontormo, Rosso Fiorentino, Andrea del Sarto (1486-1530), the first great interpreters of the "modern manner" – this exceptional Roman congeries included the Sienese Beccafumi as well as Giulio Romano (last decade of 15th century - 1546), Parmigianino (1504-1540) and Cecchino Salviati (1510-1563), to mention only some of the artists now represented in the Uffizi. The courts of Ferrara and Urbino too were vivacious centers of culture, while the Venetian painters of the early 16th century already demonstrate that poetics of landscape, that soft tonalism which was to be a salient characteristic throughout the century, up to Titian and beyond, to Tintoretto (1518-1594), Bassano (1510/15-1592) and Veronese (1528-1588).

On the opposite page,
Raphael,
Madonna of the Goldfinch,
tempera on wood,
107 x 77.2 cm,
c. 1505-1506.
[ROOM 66]

Michelangelo Buonarroti,
Doni Tondo
(*Holy Family with the Infant St. John the Baptist*),
tempera on wood,
diam. 120 cm,
(without the frame),
c. 1506-1508.
[ROOM 35]

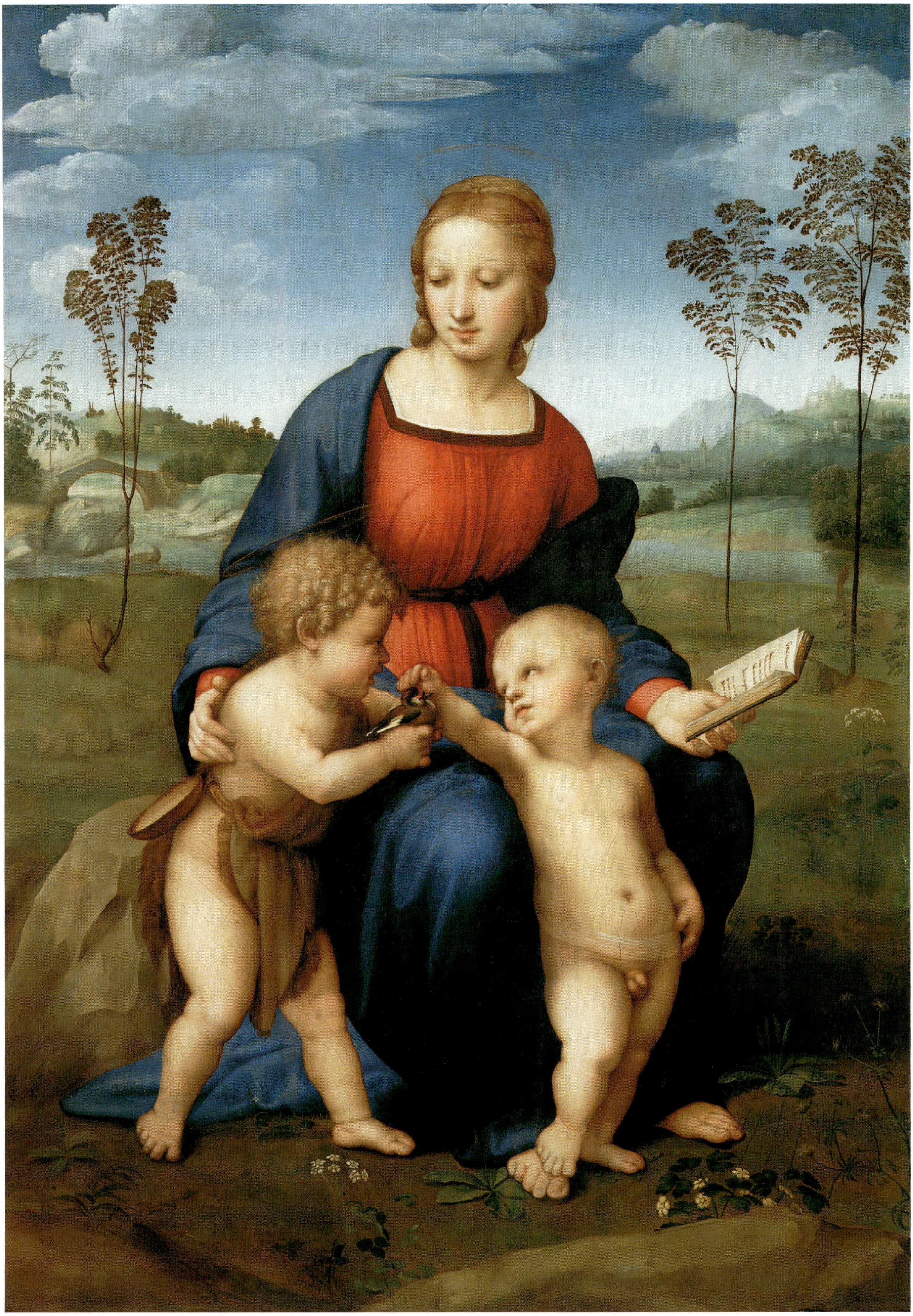

Andrea del Sarto,
Madonna of the Harpies,
tempera on wood,
207 x 178 cm, 1517.
[ROOM 58]

Mariotto Albertinelli,
Visitation,
oil on wood,
232.5 x 146.5 cm, 1503.
[ROOM 35]

Believed for a long time a painting on wood by itself, the *Musical Cherub* by Rosso Fiorentino (1494-1540), investigated with reflectography, is probably the fragment of an altarpiece with the Virgin and Saints, of which, however, no other trace remains. The cherub probably sat on steps, indicated by parallel incisions on the surface of the painting. Down towards the right the signature (partially rubbed off) became legible, as did the date, perhaps painted by Rosso himself on the already separate fragment of the panel. The development of this great artist, whose mode of expression was so unique in the art world of his time, often encountered that of artists who were strangers or "eccentrics", thanks his many journeys to other Italian cities, and his final destination at the Fontainebleau court of King Francis I in France. In the same years Pontormo (1494-1556) paints the *Portrait of Cosimo the Elder*. Portrayed in profile, as in a humanist medallion, the "Pater Patriae" has next to him the Medici emblem of a *broncone*, a broken branch with a new shoot hinting at the continuity of his descendants: the shoot is the future Duke Cosimo I, born from a cadet branch of the family in 1519, when after the Duke of Urbino's death the family lineage risked extinction.

Rosso Fiorentino,
Musical Cherub,
oil on wood,
39 x 47 cm,
1521.
[ROOM 60]

On the opposite page,
Pontormo,
Portrait of Cosimo the Elder,
oil on wood,
86 x 65 cm,
1519-1520.
[ROOM 61]

COSMO MED
ICES·P·P·
P

Bronzino (Agnolo di Cosimo),
Portrait of Lucrezia Panciatichi,
oil on wood,
102 x 83.2 cm, c. 1541.
[ROOM 64]

In the *Portrait of Lucrezia Panciatichi*, Lucrezia's melancholy gaze has struck the imagination of writers such as Vernon Lee and Henry James. Lying against her sumptuous dress, the gold and enamel plaques of her necklace bear the words *amour dure sans fin*, which may be read in circular manner: *dure sans fin amour, sans fin amour dure*.

Commissioned in 1538 from the Venetian master Titian (c. 1488 - 1576) by Guidubaldo della Rovere, the Duke of Urbino, the *Venus of Urbino* is one of the most famous erotic images of all time, a cultural icon. A young girl with blond hair flowing loosely over her shoulders looks knowingly but allusively at the spectator. She is completely naked, lying on a luxurious bed with rumpled sheets; her left hand resting over the pubic area as if to hide it is in fact ambiguously inviting. In her right hand she holds a small posy of roses, a symbol of love reiterated by the myrtle plant on the window-sill. The little dog sleeping on the bed, symbolises fidelity, a tender and reassuring note in the scene; this carries on into the background, where two maid-servants are looking for clothes in a rich bridal chest, in a fading sunset.

Titian,
Venus of Urbino,
oil on canvas,
119 x 165 cm,
1538.
[ROOM 28]

46

On the opposite page,
Parmigianino,
*The Madonna
of the Long Neck*
(*Madonna with Child,
Angels and St. Jerome*),
oil on wood,
219 x 135 cm,
c. 1534-1539.
[ROOM 29]

Paolo Veronese,
*Holy Family
with Saint Catherine
and the Infant St. John*,
oil on canvas,
86 x 122 cm,
c. 1562-1565.
[ROOM 31]

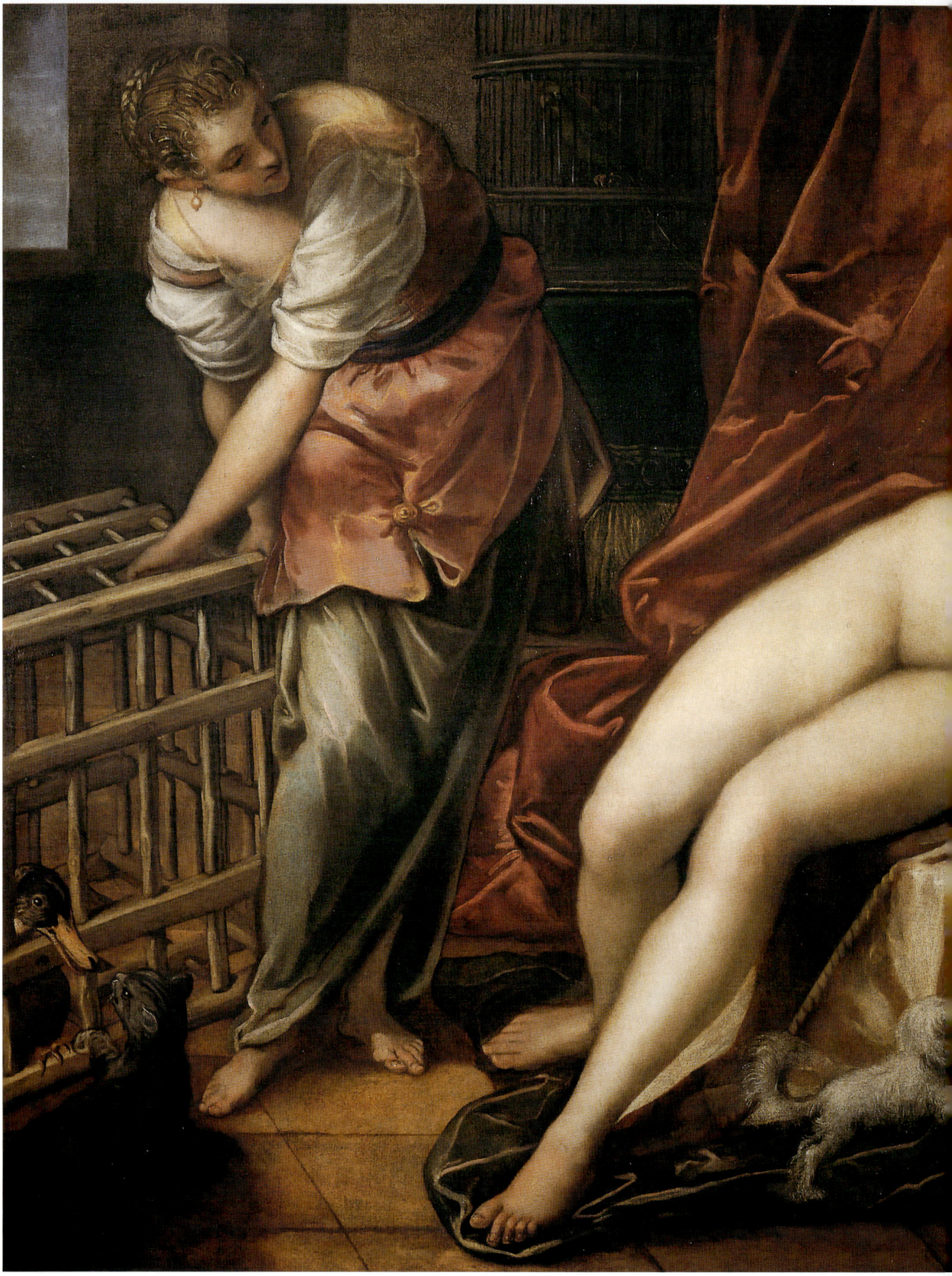

Jacopo Tintoretto,
Leda and the Swan,
oil on canvas,
167 x 221 cm,
c. 1550-1560.
[ROOM 32]

The XVII and the XVIII Centuries

The large group of 17th and 18th century paintings in the Uffizi is highly important to the history of the collections formed by the Medici and Lorraine families. These collections, which include portraits, still lifes, genre and religious scenes, are now placed mainly in the Vasari Corridor. At present it is hard to describe them in diachronic order, but in the meantime some of these were transferred in March 2004 to the first floor of the museum, where they were placed in the renovated rooms (east wing).

The Medici had a real fondness for "foreigners". In addition to the magnificent paintings of Rubens – one of the artists most appreciated and sought after by the noble family – such as the *Triumph* (p. 57), works by others, including Van Dyck (1599-1641), Velázquez (1599-1660), Rembrandt (1606-1669) and Goya, arrived in the collection. As regards Caravaggio, who decidedly renewed 17th century painting in the naturalistic sense, it should be noted that the artist never worked in Florence. The Medici received his paintings as gifts considered at the time both precious and highly unusual, such as the *Head of Medusa* (p. 4), depicted with startling realism in the act of screaming.

Judith and Holophernes was painted by Artemisia Gentileschi, the most famous woman painter of the 17th century, for Cosimo II de' Medici. Judith, a traditional example of virtue and chastity, is shown here about to decapitate her despised Assyrian enemy whom she has tricked by seduction, while safeguarding her own purity. Due to its violence, the work was confined "to a dark corner" in the Pitti Palace and after the death of Cosimo II, Artemisia had to recur to the mediation of Galileo to obtain her stipulated recompense.

Giuseppe Maria Crespi,
Cupid and Psyche,
oil on canvas,
130 x 215 cm, c. 1709.
[ROOM 45]

On the opposite page,
Artemisia Gentileschi,
Judith and Holophernes,
oil on canvas,
199 x 162.5 cm, 1620.
[CARAVAGGIO'S ROOM]

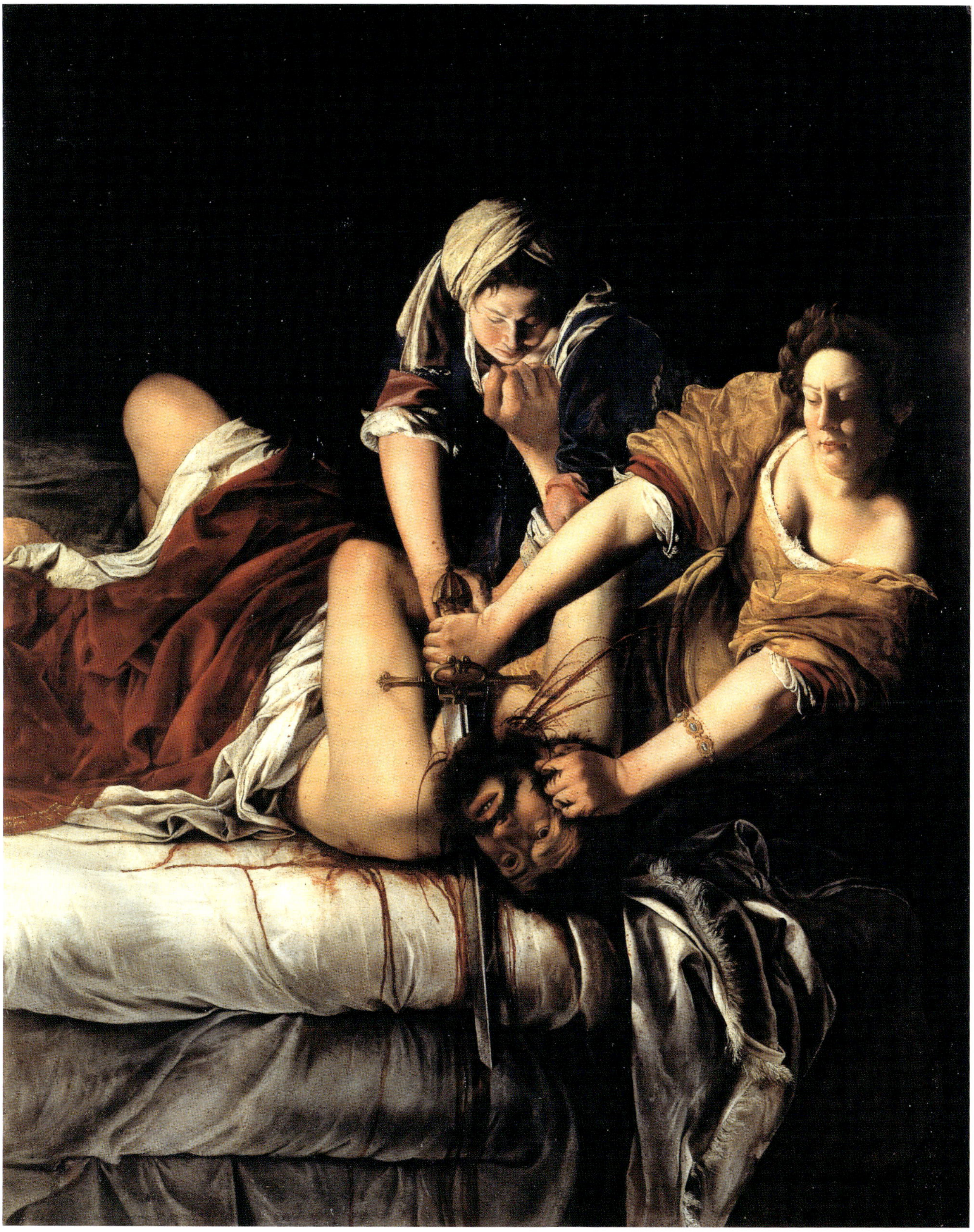

Caravaggio,
Bacchus,
oil on canvas,
95 x 85 cm,
1597-1598.
[CARAVAGGIO'S ROOM]

Caravaggio,
Sacrifice of Isaac,
oil on canvas,
104 x 135 cm,
1601-1602, whole and detail
on the following pages.
[CARAVAGGIO'S ROOM]

Taken out of storage in 1916, the *Bacchus* was attributed to Caravaggio (1571 - 1610) by Roberto Longhi. It is now generally believed that the *Bacchus* was painted for the highly cultured Cardinal Francesco Maria Del Monte, whose guest the young painter was starting from 1595. Del Monte may have then donated the *Bacchus* to Ferdinando I de' Medici, known to have received from him the *Medusa*. It has been hypothesized that the adolescent face of the wine god is that of the young Sicilian painter Mario Monnitti, who had lived with Caravaggio for some time in Rome. The meaning of the painting is hotly debated, filled as it is with symbols, even of esoteric nature. The figure of Bacchus, recurrently used by the painter, could be an allegory for Christ, offering the cup of Salvation. Regardless of its real meaning, the work is imbued with sensuality and crude realism: reddened cheeks, swollen lips, dirty fingernails, and worm-eaten, half-rotten fruit.

In the *Sacrifice of Isaac* by Caravaggio, an angel is stopping Abraham, about to sacrifice his son Isaac in obedience to God's terrible command. Beside the head of the boy, who is screaming desperately, appears the ram sent by God to take his place in the sacrifice. While in the Biblical text the angel speaks to Abraham from the sky, here he descends to stay his hand directly. The scene, painted with fine strokes of light against a landscape showing a serene Venetian influence, prefigures the sacrifice of Christ and symbolizes obedience and faith in keeping with the climate of renewed spirituality of the time.

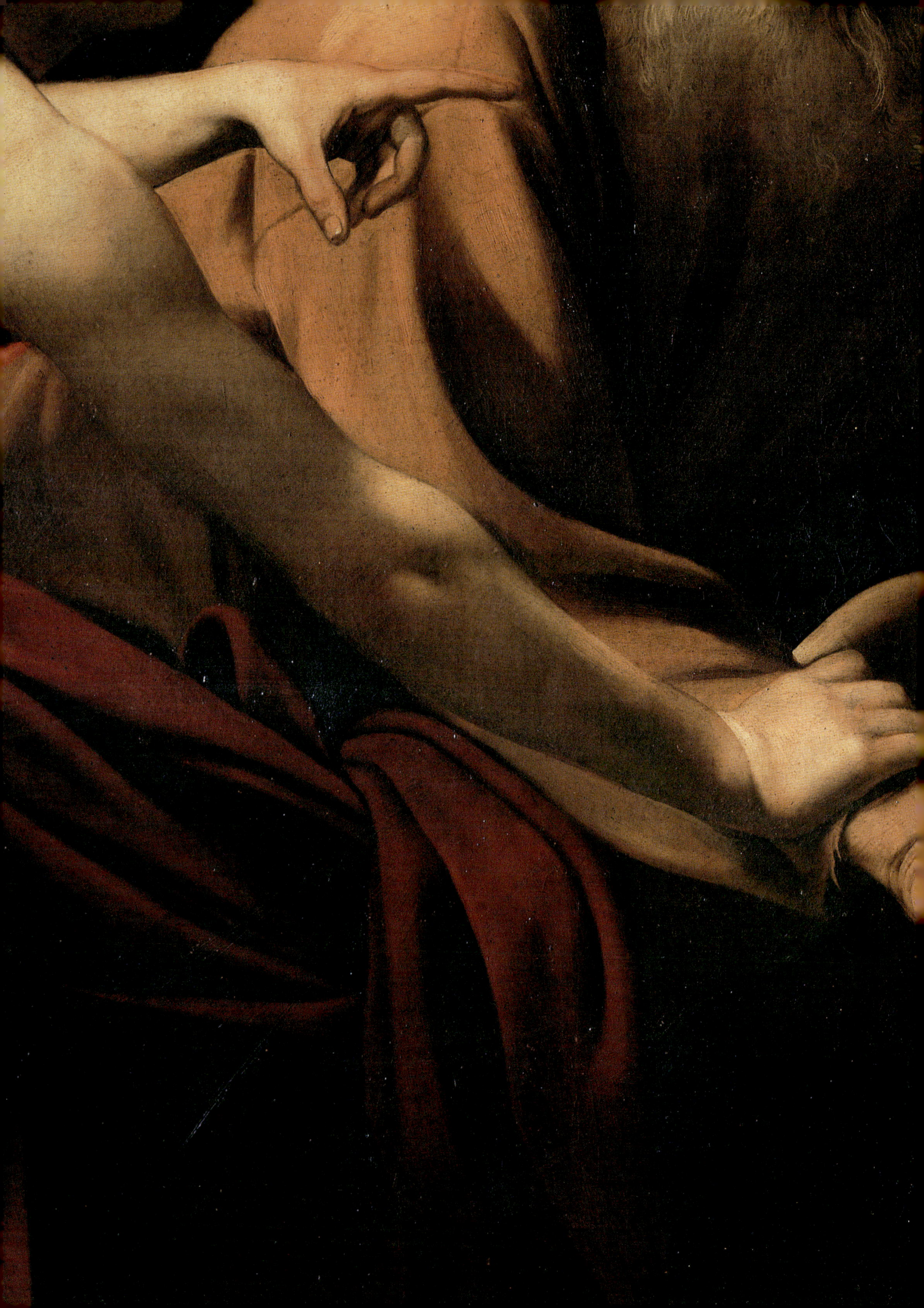

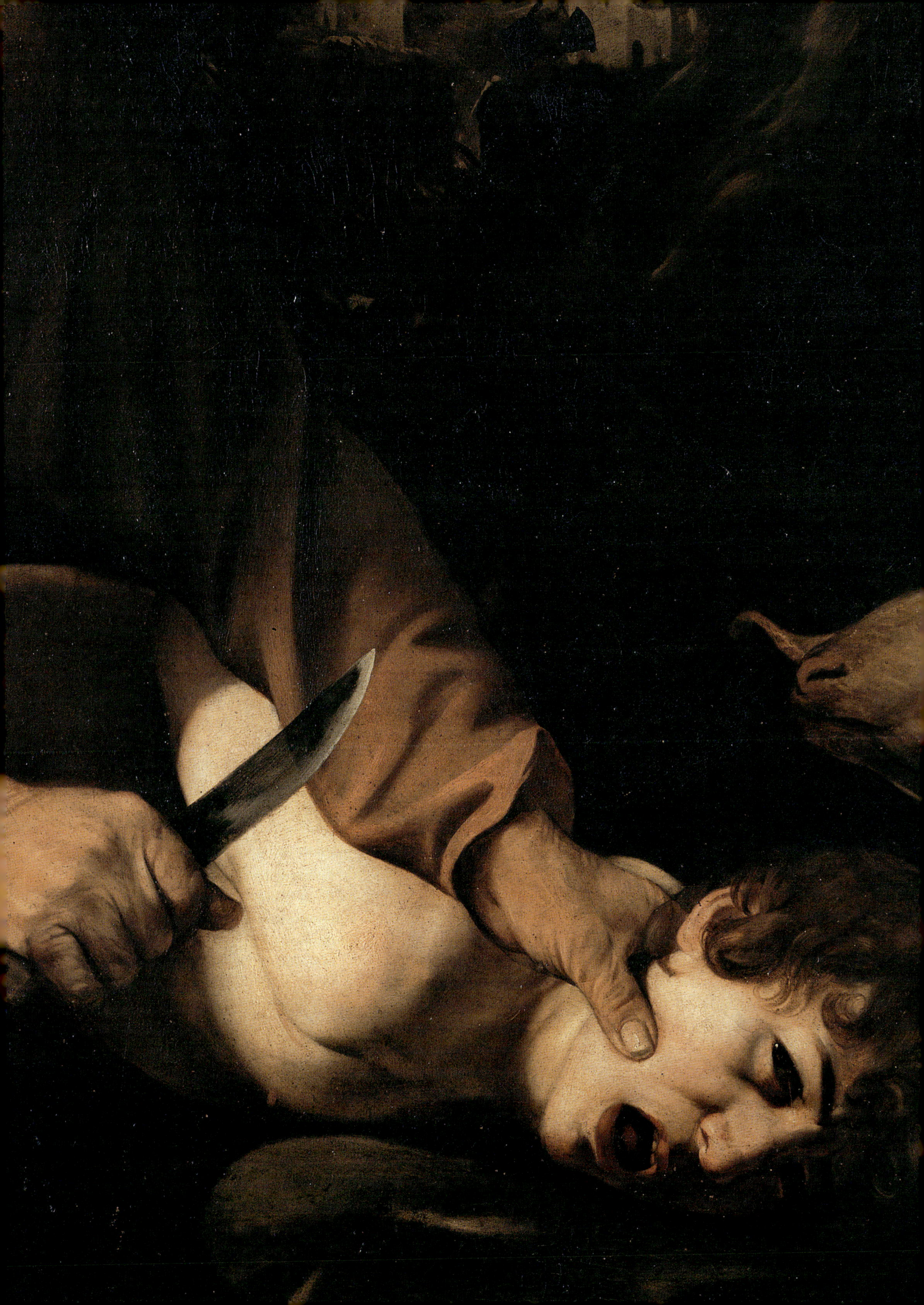

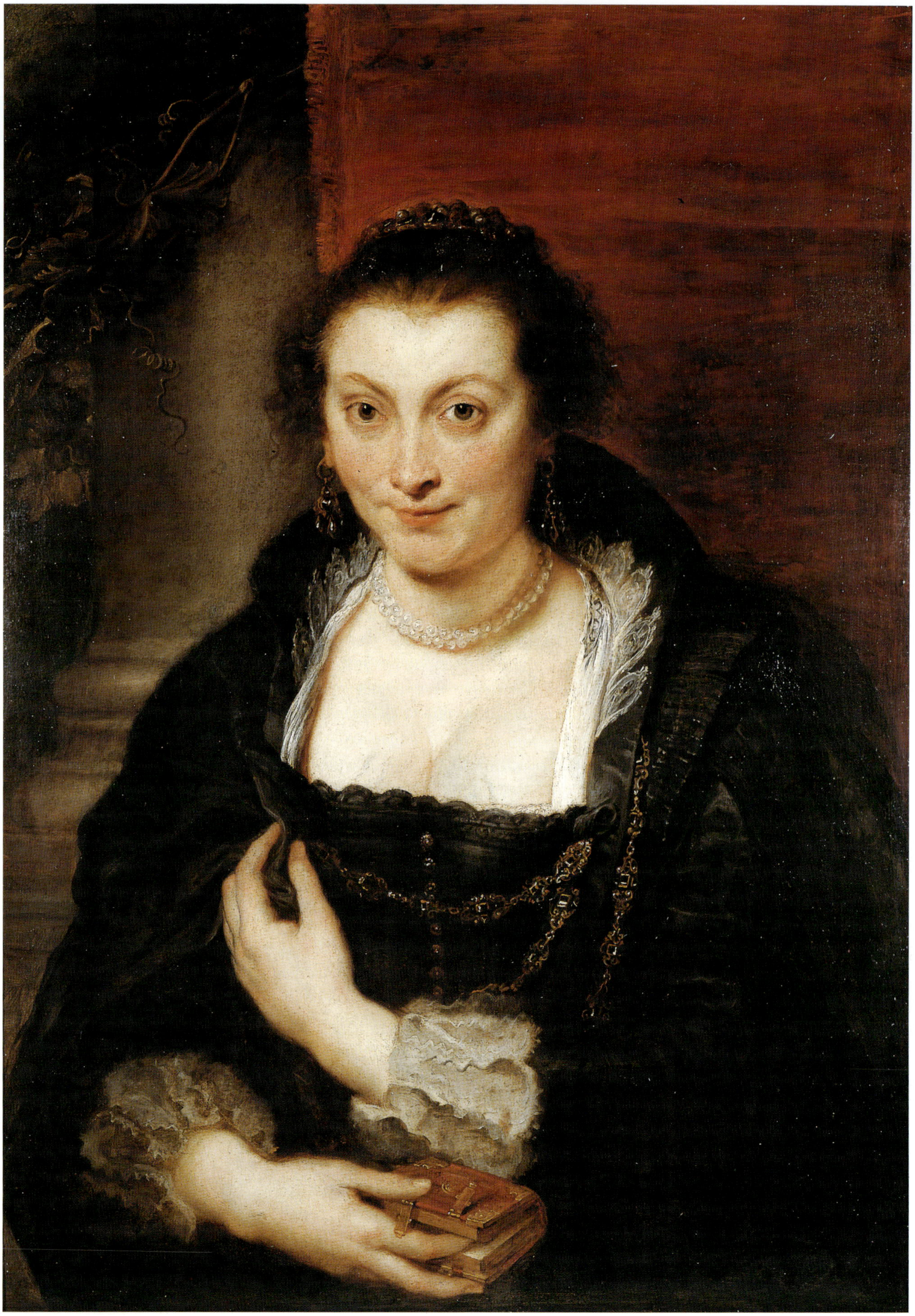

The *Triumph* by Pieter Paul Rubens (1577-1640) is an enormous canvas inspired by the life of Henri IV, which formed part – like the *Battle*, also in the Uffizi – of a series left unfinished in 1630. Maria de' Medici, widow of the King of France, had commissioned the Flemish artist, who may have been present at the royal wedding, celebrated by proxy in Florence in 1600, to paint a commemorative series of battles, sieges and triumphs of the King of France. The series was to accompany the scenes from the life of the Queen, painted by Rubens from 1622 to 1625 for the Luxembourg Palace. Diplomatic and political problems (Maria was confined to Compiègne and then exiled) prevented the second project from being carried out. After the painter's death the canvases now in the Uffizi went to the collection of the Antwerp Canon Fréderic Lancelot, at Cambrai. Although the painter Charles Le Brun tried to buy them for the King of France, it was Apollonio Bassetti, secretary of Cosimo III, who managed to obtain them. In 1687 they arrived from Antwerp at the port of Livorno, wound in great rolls, and from there to Florence.

The *Portrait of Isabella Brandt*, considered one of the masterpieces of Rubens portraiture, was donated in 1705, with other paintings, by the Palatine Elector of the Rhine Johann Wilhelm to his brother-in-law, Grand Prince Ferdinando de' Medici, brother of Anna Maria Luisa. The portrait, highly appreciated by the Grand Prince, was displayed in the Villa Medicea of Poggio a Caiano. On December 10, 1705 Ferdinando wrote his brother-in-law to thank him for the Rubens painting, which "surpasses the imagination and is a prodigy of that famous brush".

On the opposite page,
Pieter Paul Rubens,
Portrait of Isabella Brandt,
oil on wood,
86 x 62 cm,
c. 1625.
[ROOM 55]

Pieter Paul Rubens,
Triumph,
oil on canvas,
380 x 692 cm,
1627-1630.
[ROOM 42]

Antoon van Dyck,
The *Emperor Charles V on Horseback*,
oil on canvas,
191 x 123 cm,
c. 1620.
[ROOM 55]

On the opposite page,
Diego Velázquez,
Philip IV of Spain on Horseback,
oil on canvas,
338 x 267 cm,
c. 1645.
[ROOM 41]

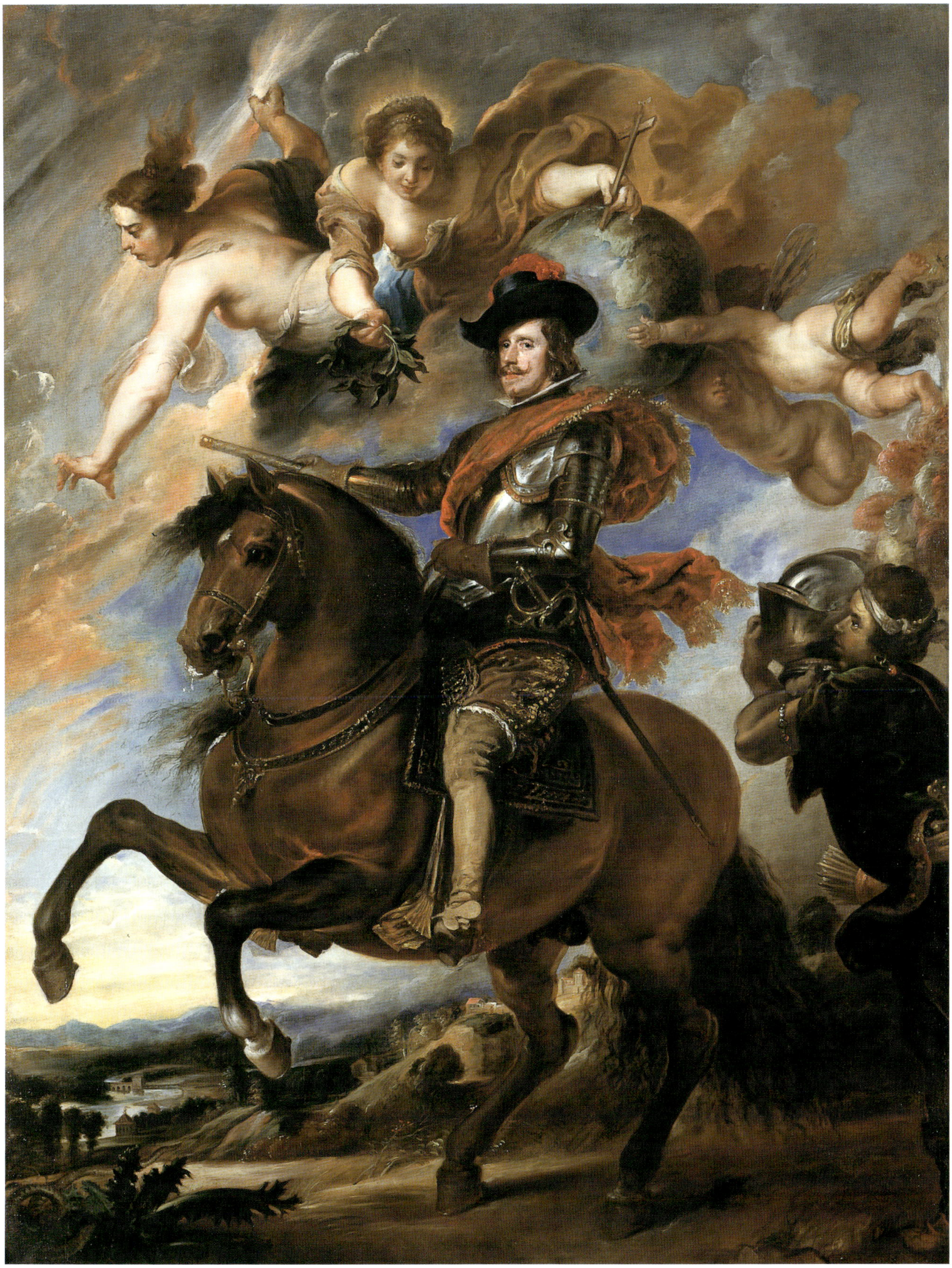

The *Presumed Portrait of Maria Adelaide of France dressed in Turkish costume* was painted by Jean-Etienne Liotard (1702-1789), a painter of French origin from Geneva, a master of the portrait set in an Oriental scenario, known after his stay in Constantinople (1738-1742) as the "peintre turc". The charm of the composition springs from the pose of the figure and the contrast between the brilliant, intense greens of the divan and the sultan's cap and the fine, light layers of fabric in the Turkish gown.

Maria Teresa, Countess of Chinchón painted by Francisco Goya (1746-1828), is the unfortunate daughter of his patron, the Infante Don Luis de Borbon. Her unhappy life, is not yet to be guessed from this gently smiling portrait. It is a glowing image that reveals both Goya's artistic intelligence and his sympathy for his model. The profile of the young woman appears again in the medallion on her wrist, through the expedient of the "painting within a painting" so dear to Spanish painters.

Jean-Etienne Liotard,
Presumed Portrait of Maria Adelaide of France dressed in Turkish costume,
oil on canvas,
50 x 56 cm,
1753.
[ROOM 51]

On the opposite page,
Francisco Goya,
Maria Teresa, Countess of Chinchón,
220 x 140 cm,
c. 1798.
[ROOM 46]

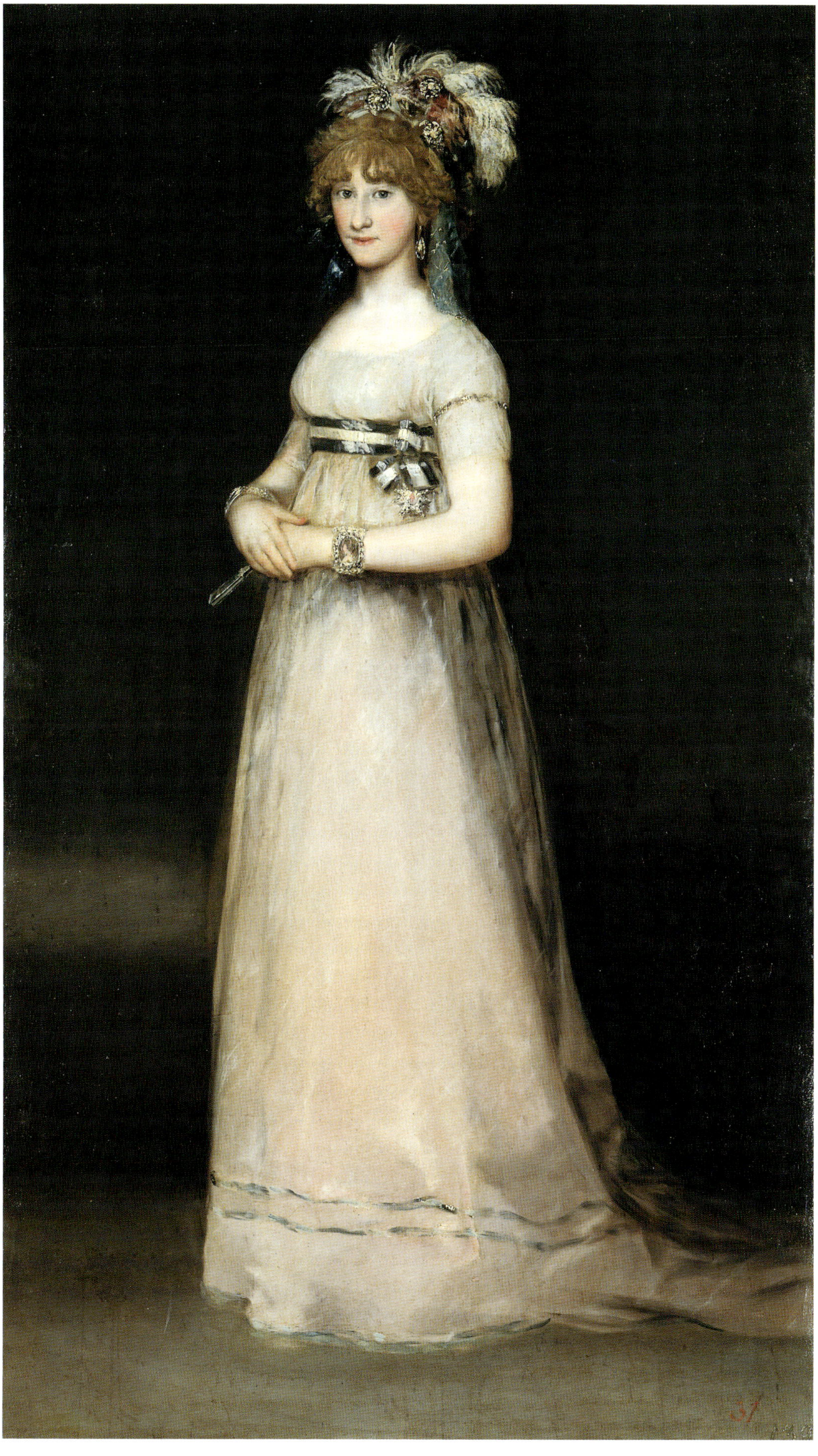

The Dutch artist Gerrit A. Berckheyde (1638-1698), is considered a forerunner of 18th century veduta painting. His painting is distinguished by a terse light, appearing also in the famous canvas of the Uffizi showing the animated square of *The Groote Markt in Haarlem*, dominated by the imposing structure of the church of St. Bavone. This composition, highly successful, was replicated in a number of variations: one in the London National Gallery, one in the Basil Kunstmuseum and another, dated 1696, in the Frans Hals Museum of Haarlem.

Gerrit A. Berckheyde,
The Groote Markt in Haarlem,
oil on canvas,
54 x 64 cm,
1693.
[ROOM 54]

Canaletto,
View of the Ducal Palace in Venezia,
oil on canvas,
51 x 83 cm,
before 1755.
[ROOM 45]

Among the most often copied vedutas of the great Venetian painter, the *View of the Ducal Palace in Venice*, formerly at Poggio Imperiale, shows the wharf and the Riva degli Schiavoni with limpid precision. For his incomparable perspective views Canaletto utilized the "camera ottica", a forerunner of today's camera, a box containing mirrors that projected, through a series of reflections, an image on a sheet, allowing the painter to copy directly from life. In the Uffizi canvas the foreground is dominated by gondolas and boats with figures intent on rowing or throwing mooring ropes. In the background of the Uffizi painting can be seen the Mint, the Old Library, Ducal Palace and Dandolo Palace.

Information

Galleria degli Uffizi
piazzale degli Uffizi, Florence, Italy

Open Tuesday to Sunday 8.15-18.50
Closed Mondays, Christmas Day, New Year's Day, May 1st
tel. +39 055 2388651

Bookings: Firenze Musei, tel. +39 055 294883

www.uffizi.firenze.it

Photograph credits:
Archivio Giunti; Archivio Giunti / photo Nicola Grifoni, Florence;
Archivio Giunti / photo Rabatti & Domingie, Florence;
Lorenzo Mennonna, Florence; Antonio Quattrone, Florence.

Babouchka

Une légende russe racontée par Henri Troyat
illustrée par Olivier Tallec

Père Castor ■ Flammarion

© 2005 Flammarion
ISBN : 978-2-0816-2774-1 – ISSN : 1768-2061

Assise au coin du feu, le dos rond, les mains sur les genoux,
Babouchka écoute le vent d'hiver qui hurle dans la plaine.
Il accourt de loin, s'écrase contre la porte,
jette des étoiles de neige à la vitre noire,
s'engouffre dans la cheminée
et secoue furieusement la flamme du foyer,
qui se cabre et qui ronfle.

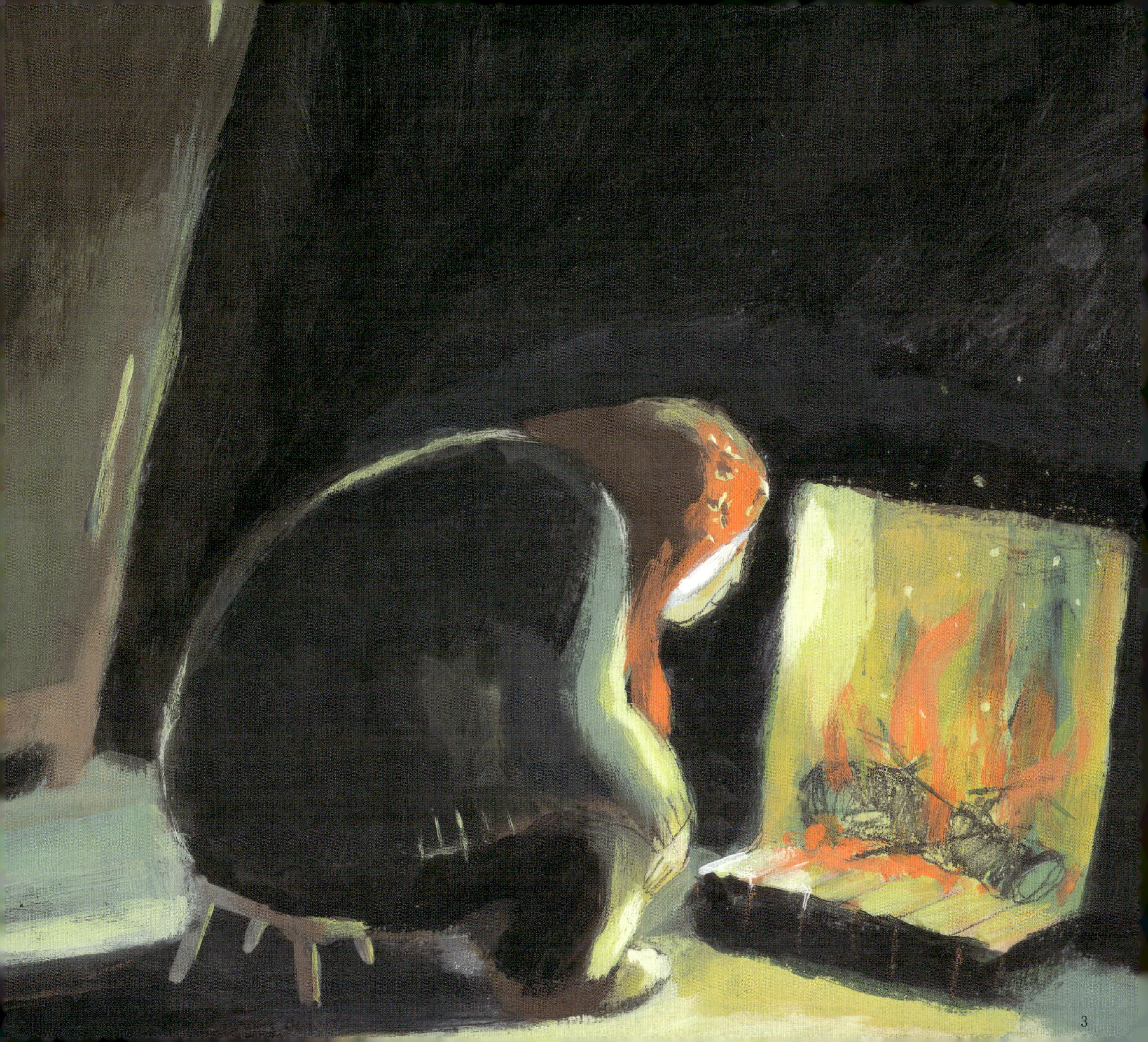

4

Malgré ce tumulte, Babouchka n'a pas peur,
il fait si bon dans l'isba, quand, dehors,
tout n'est que froid, ténèbres et violence !
Et puis, elle n'est pas seule :
son vieux chien noir, Joutchok, tout velu, tout perclus,
grogne de bien-être dans un panier,
tandis que sa chatte tigrée,
Kissa, se lèche le plastron avec une application maniaque.
Soudain, Joutchok ouvre un œil, le poil de Kissa se hérisse.
Quelqu'un frappe à la porte. En pleine nuit !
Qui est-ce donc ? Un voyageur égaré, sans doute...

Nullement troublée,
Babouchka se lève en geignant de son tabouret
(« Ah ! mes vieilles jambes ! »),
prend une chandelle et pousse le verrou de bois.
L'ouragan couche la flamme du lumignon,
mais ne peut l'éteindre ;
Dans la clarté dansante, apparaissent
trois étrangers, grands et barbus.
Leurs vêtements sont couverts de neige,
les poils de leur menton sont raides et blancs
comme ces longs glaçons qui pendent aux gouttières,
une perle liquide tremble au bout de leur nez rouge,
des diamants brillent dans leurs yeux avivés par le froid et,
tout autour de leurs épaules,
tourbillonnent des flocons légers tel un duvet de cygne.

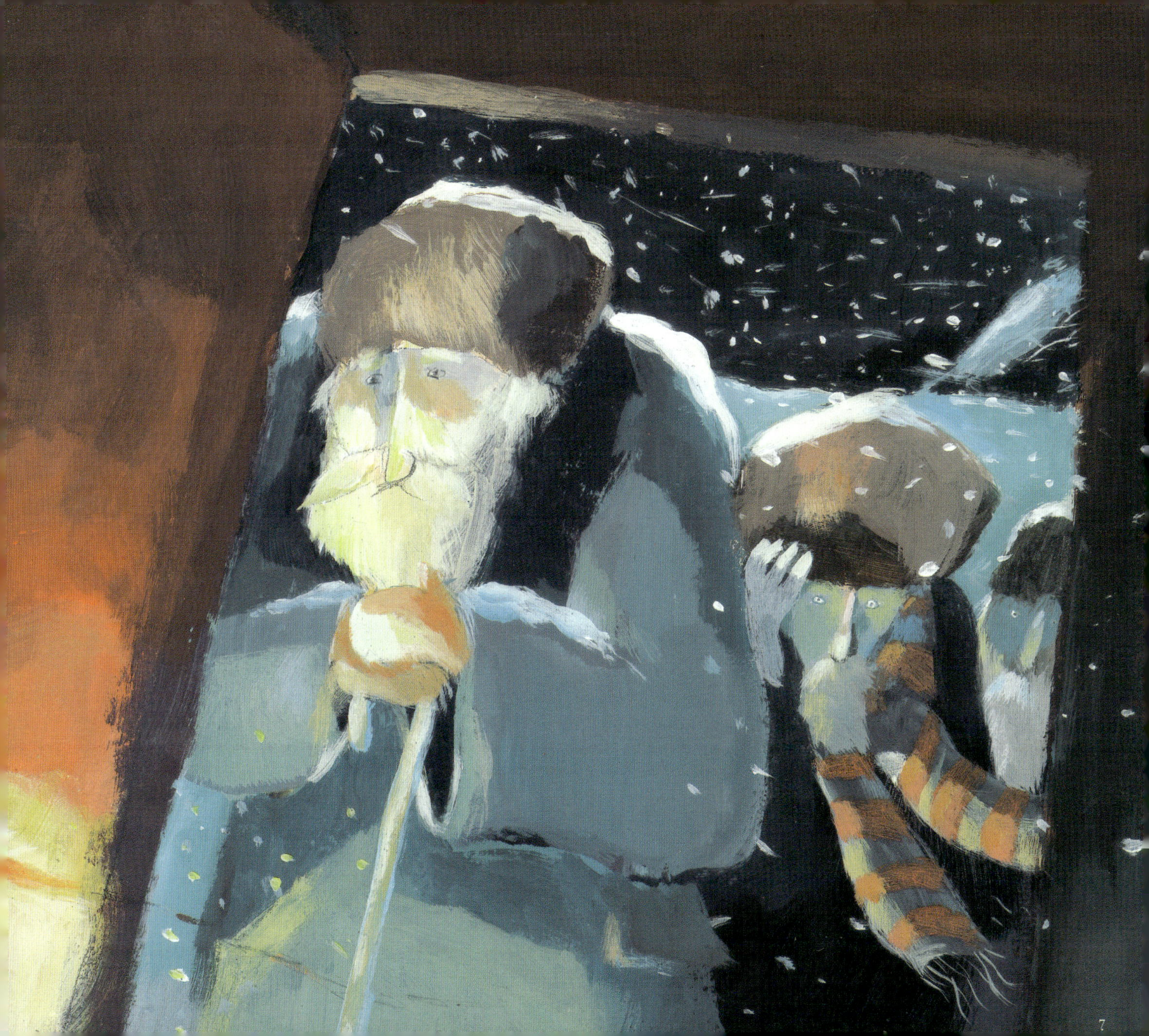

Le chien grogne en retroussant les babines,
la chatte souffle de colère, puis, – comme c'est étrange ! –
tous deux s'apaisent, courbent l'échine et vont se frotter
amicalement contre les jambes des nouveaux venus.
– Babouchka, dit l'un d'eux (et, tandis qu'il parle,
son haleine sort en vapeur de sa bouche),
Babouchka, nous venons de très loin et nous voulons,
en passant, t'apprendre une grande nouvelle.
Cette nuit nous est né un petit Prince,
qui régnera sur l'univers.
Nous lui apportons des cadeaux.
Mais nous ne savons pas au juste où il loge.
Veux-tu nous accompagner ?
Partons ensemble à sa recherche...

9

Sur le seuil, Babouchka frissonne.
Elle voudrait bien voir le petit Prince, le fils du roi.
Mais la nuit est si froide, le vent si brutal,
il y a tant de neige sur les chemins, elle est trop vieille !...
Et puis, elle ne peut laisser Joutchok et Kissa
seuls à la maison. Que deviendront-ils sans elle ? Qui les nourrira ?
À moins qu'elle ne les emmène avec elle ?...
Pour gagner du temps, elle dit aux visiteurs :
– Entrez donc vous chauffer, vous reposer un peu.
Je vais réfléchir, peser le pour et le contre...
Mais ils secouent la tête, tous les trois ensemble,
comme tirés par une même ficelle :
– Non, Babouchka, nous sommes trop pressés !

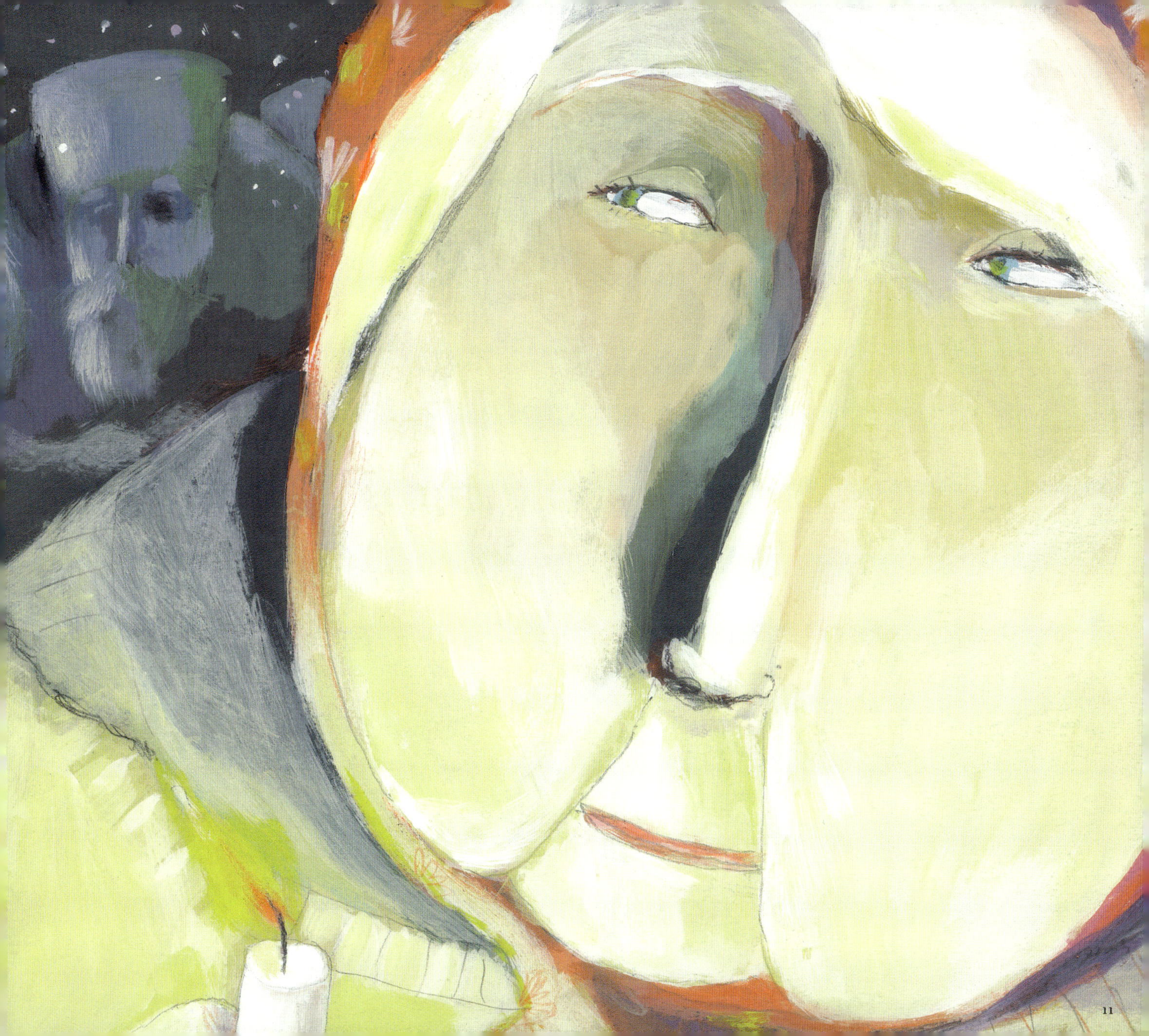

Et ils s'en vont dans la nuit,
  marchant l'un derrière l'autre, les pieds lourds,
  la barbe au vent, parmi la neige qui tournoie.

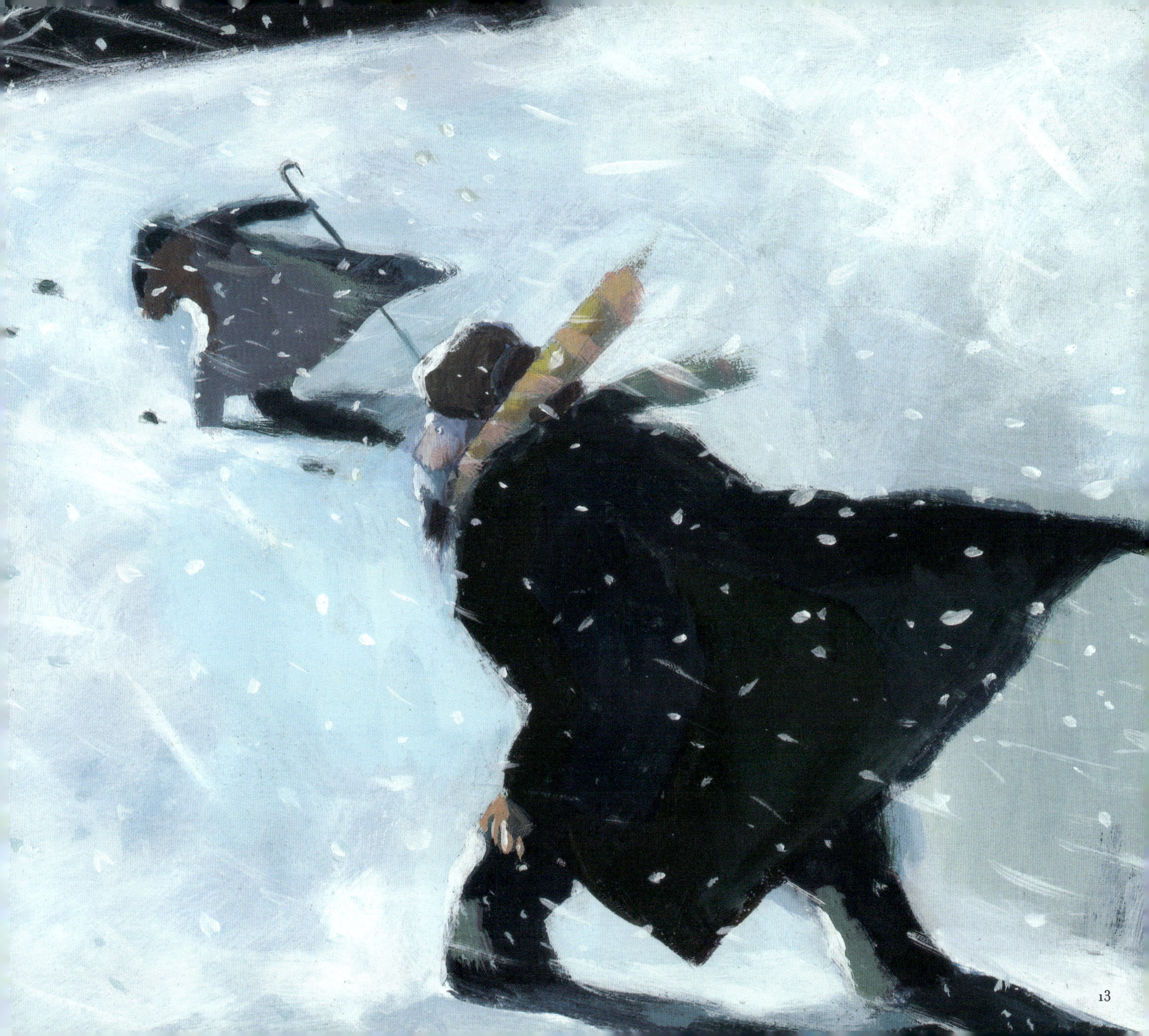

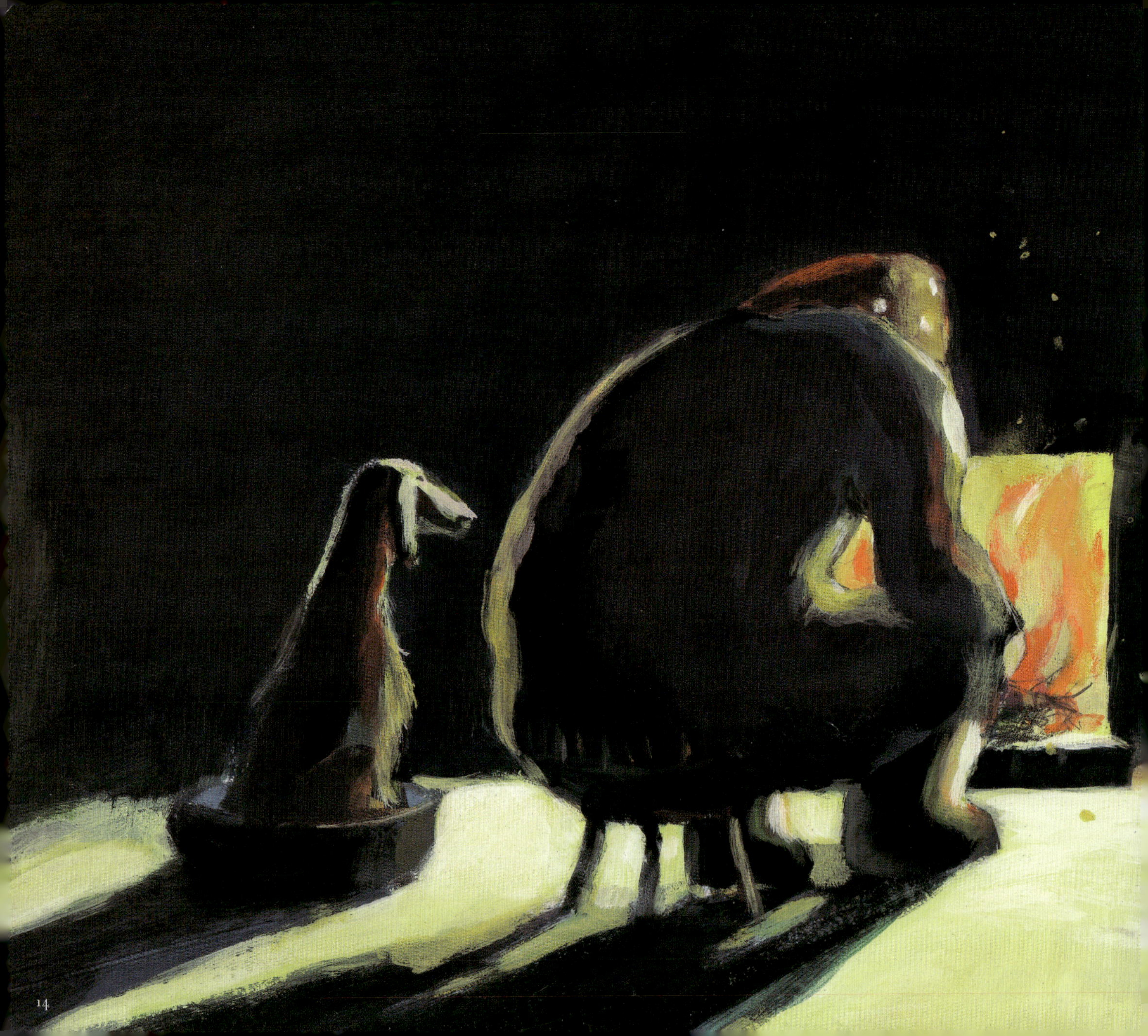

Restée seule, Babouchka se rassied devant le feu,
entre son chien et sa chatte,
tend ses vieilles mains veineuses à la flamme
et songe, l'esprit engourdi :
« Je ne leur ai pas demandé qui était le petit Prince,
ni comment ils avaient appris sa naissance,
ni où ils espéraient le découvrir !... Suis-je sotte !...
Quel dommage !... Demain je me lèverai très tôt ;
je partirai avec Joutchok et Kissa ;
les bêtes ont plus de flair que les humains ;
elles m'aideront à retrouver les trois étrangers ;
je les rattraperai ; je marcherai derrière eux ;
j'apporterai au petit Prince des cadeaux dans un sac...
Justement, j'ai colorié des noix pour passer le temps !
Ce projet enchante Babouchka,
et elle s'assoupit, assise sur son tabouret,
un sourire de fête sur son visage ridé.

Aux premiers rayons du soleil,
elle est déjà sur le sentier neigeux, un bâton à la main,
un sac plein de noix coloriées sur le dos.
Joutchok court devant elle,
la queue en panache, le museau fureteur,
Kissa marche sur ses talons, la moustache hérissée,
la patte molle et circonspecte.

17

À chaque paysan qu'elle croise,
Babouchka demande s'il sait où habite le petit Prince.
Mais nul ne peut lui répondre.
Les uns haussent les épaules, d'autres lui rient au nez,
d'autres encore la traitent de folle.
Cela ne la chagrine pas du tout.
Elle sait bien que les fous ce sont ceux qui doutent !
Et elle repart en boitillant, toujours souriante,
avec son chien qui jappe de joie
et sa chatte qui miaule de tristesse.
La trace de leurs pas se perd en zigzags
dans la campagne blanche.

19

Ainsi, parfois, la nuit de Noël,
quand une neige épaisse couvre les champs,
une très vieille femme passe de village en village.
Son visage fripé penche vers le sol.
Elle tient un bâton à la main et porte un sac sur le dos.
Un chat et un chien l'accompagnent.
Ils ont l'air aussi âgés qu'elle, transis, raidis, fatigués.

21

Elle choisit une maison, y entre à pas feutrés,
pendant que tout le monde dort,
traverse des chambres obscures
et se penche sur un lit où repose un enfant
aux yeux clos, au souffle tranquille.
Il émane d'elle un parfum de gel et de citron.
Des larmes d'argent brillent dans ses prunelles fixes.
Longtemps elle contemple le tendre visage
enfoui dans un oreiller.
Enfin, elle secoue la tête et murmure :
– Ce n'est pas le petit Prince.
Il faut que j'aille plus loin...

23

Et elle s'en va, légère, insaisissable,
laissant dans la chambre
un simple jouet et une bouffée d'air froid.